D1635017

Esther Morgan was born in Kidderminster, Worcestershire. She first started writing poetry while working as a volunteer at the Wordsworth Trust in Grasmere, Cumbria. After completing an MA in Creative Writing at the University of East Anglia in 1997, she taught on UEA's undergraduate creative writing course and for the Department of Continuing Education. After a teaching exchange to Edith Cowan University in Perth, Australia, Morgan returned to UEA where she edited four editions of the poetry anthology *Reactions*.

She was awarded an Eric Gregory Award in 1998 and her first collection, *Beyond Calling Distance*, was published by Bloodaxe in 2001. It won the Aldeburgh First Collection Prize and was shortlisted for the John Llewellyn Rhys Prize. Her second collection, *The Silence Living in Houses* (Bloodaxe Books, 2005), was largely inspired by her time caretaking a run-down Edwardian house in Goring-on-Thames, Oxfordshire. In 2010 she won the Bridport Poetry Prize for her poem 'This Morning', included in her third collection *Grace* (Bloodaxe Books, 2011), which is a Poetry Book Society Recommendation.

As well as freelance teaching and editing work, Esther Morgan is currently Historic Recordings Manager for the Poetry Archive, the world's largest online collection of poets reading their own work: www.poetryarchive.org. After four years in Oxfordshire, she moved back to Norfolk.

ESTHER MORGAN

GRACE

BLOODAXE BOOKS

Copyright © Esther Morgan 2011

ISBN: 978 1 85224 918 2

First published 2011 by
Bloodaxe Books Ltd,
Highgreen,
Tarset,
Northumberland NE48 1RP.

www.bloodaxebooks.com
For further information about Bloodaxe titles
please visit our website or write to
the above address for a catalogue.

Supported by
**ARTS COUNCIL
ENGLAND**

LEGAL NOTICE

All rights reserved. No part of this book may be
reproduced, stored in a retrieval system, or
transmitted in any form, or by any means, electronic,
mechanical, photocopying, recording or otherwise,
without prior written permission from Bloodaxe Books Ltd.

Requests to publish work from this book
must be sent to Bloodaxe Books Ltd.

Esther Morgan has asserted her right under
Section 77 of the Copyright, Designs and Patents Act 1988
to be identified as the author of this work.

Cover design: Neil Astley & Pamela Robertson-Pearce.

Printed in Great Britain by
Bell & Bain Limited, Glasgow, Scotland.

For Livia Elsie

ACKNOWLEDGEMENTS

Acknowledgements are due to the editors of the following publications where some of these poems first appeared: *The Best British Poetry 2011* (Salt Publishing, 2011), *Did I Tell You? 131 Poems for Children in Need* (Word Aid, 2010), *Images of Women* (Arrowhead Press, 2006), *Ink, Sweat and Tears, In the Mix* (Cambridge University Press, 2007), *Magma, Poetry Review, Seam, Smiths Knoll* and *Spring* (Gatehouse Press, 2009).

'This Morning' won the 2010 Bridport Prize, 'Garbo Among Us' won third prize in the 2010 *Mslexia* poetry competition while 'Short-hold' was shortlisted in the same competition. 'The Dew Artist' was shortlisted for the Larkin and East Riding Poetry Prize 2011.

In addition I'd like to thank the following whose advice and encouragement has been invaluable in helping to shape this collection: Martin Figura and Helen Ivory for organising our regular poetry get-togethers and the members of the group – Joanna Guthrie, Andrea Holland, Matthew Howard, Andrew McDonnell and Tom Warner; Polly Clark and all the great women poets on the Cove Park retreat, September 2010; Jo Emeney, Brian Johnstone, Esther Menon, Helen Oswald, Fiona Robyn, Sibyl Ruth, and Heidi Williamson. Thank you to my friends and family for their continuing support, and to my husband, Kelvyn, for the past and the future.

CONTENTS

Grace

You've been living for this for weeks
without knowing it:

the moment the house empties like a city in August
so completely
it forgets you exist.

Light withdraws slowly
is almost gone before you notice.

In the stillness, everything becomes itself:
the circle of white plates on the kitchen table
the serious chairs that attend them

even the roses on the papered walls
seem to open a little wider.

It looks simple: the glass vase holding
whatever is offered –
cut flowers, or the thought of them –

simple, though not easy
this waiting without hunger in the near dark
for what you may be about to receive.

*   *   *

Among Women

One evening I came back home
and everything was just as I'd left it –

except the bowls gleamed with a new knowledge,
the cat wore his yellow gaze like a mask,

and I sensed the house had been visited –
wings unfurling like ferns in the quiet air.

I was blessed with children anyway,
I shook my life out like a cloth,

and perhaps there is a purpose after all
in not being chosen:

the minute my clock has never regained,
sunlight in the guest room climbing its ladder of dust.

This Year, Next Year, Sometime, Never

Stepping in from the brightness,
the room was shady and cool as a larder,

the table clothed like an altar
and laid as if for a different life.

Finding the tongue still lithe
and moving in my head,

I sat and ate my fill –
the day old bread thinly sliced and buttered

the late-summer plums in their staining juice
answering a hunger I'd never known until then.

I hardly need to tell you this –
the sharpness following the sweetness,

the bruise-coloured flesh,
then the clock of stones.

But for a moment
I felt my work here was completed –

galaxies of light blazing
in the mirror's bevelled edge,

the children in their grubby white shirts
gravitating slowly towards home.

Epiphany

I've been doing this ever since I was a girl –
    stepping into a moment

like an empty platform
    or a summer garden

just before the dew has lifted –
    as if I could dare you to appear.

They say not being given
    what we pray for

is also an answer: the blue sky at dawn
    with its wafer of moon,

the embankment buddleia
    burning with admirals.

Waiting Places

They seem so nondescript – these quiet shelters
and sidings where we idle like children
      for lifts, for buses and trains, for something
      to carry us away;

these cracks in our lives
where Traveller's Joy takes root,
      turning into Old Man's Beard as we wonder
      what to do with our evenings.

Week after week the grey rag flaps
invisibly, snagged in the bare branches,
      the girl last seen in jeans, a red T-shirt's
      still missing.

What if one hazy afternoon,
Greensleeves drifting from across the park,
      this Rorschach of spilt paint on the pavement,
      opened its wings?

The Nature of Things

An ordinary hour –
    hot in the shade
        the sour smell of privet

from overgrown front gardens,
    the children drowsy as flies
        in the long glass classrooms.

The traffic clears and in the gap
    the thought occurs
        like birdsong –

At this moment
    no one is thinking of me
        or even knows I'm here –

not your husband
    tapping gently at his keys,
        not your daughter

laying out clothes for the evening,
    not a single friend or relation,
        distant or close.

A word now from a stranger
    and you'd follow without question,
        your bag of bread and milk

left unattended in the sun.
    The green man shines,
        no one crosses

and what arrives instead
    through a haze of pollen and light
        is a voice telling you again

never to go up
　　or down the stairs
　　　　without carrying something,

that it's the nature of things
　　to be always
　　　　in the wrong place.

Blessed Art Thou

First I watched you kneading the dough,
how you put your whole body into it,
the surprising strength of your slim fingers.

Next you swept each room of the house
as if it were spring,
as if you were expecting a guest.

I couldn't tell from this if you were blessed,
except by my presence, the words I had been charged with
beginning to burn.

Sensing this, perhaps, you kept yourself busy
until there was nothing more to be done:
the vase of lilies set in the centre of the table.

Believe me, if I could have left you then,
as you stepped back to admire
the flowers' golden tongues...

but you chose that moment, at last, to rest,
your skin filmed and shining,
your warmth rising against me like bread.

I want to go back to The Angel

Why won't somebody take her?
It's only a short walk away

    across the late summer allotments
    where the dill must already be running to seed.

Meanwhile, here are *Tunes from the War* –
her head grows feathery with voices

    in a room bright as a kindergarten.
    A meal appears out of nowhere and is frightening.

Then it's time for undressing again,
though nothing's been done, nothing that should have been –

    the takings not counted and locked in the safe,
    the tables still sticky with rings.

Tomorrow they croon
like the daughter who'll always come later

    Tomorrow promises the wind across the river
    Tomorrow sing the creaking wings.

News

After all this time I'm still trying
to appear to you –

it's harder than you think,
requires a furious concentration:

like the apple you lift to your lips without looking
I've taken infinite pains to be here.

Once there was something I had to tell you –
the city we might flee to, or the name of a child,

words that could hinge our lives
like a breastbone its wings.

Even now when you ask
and I say *Nothing*

what I mean is *white flesh, a shining skin*:
that we must leave all we own this instant

as if the foretold enemy were coming –
our back door flung open hard against the brick,

the radio in the deserted kitchen
still blaring the news.

Enola Gay

She could be anybody's mother
pegging out the washing on a hot August morning,
lifting a sheet's saintly dazzle to the line.

The day stretches in front of her stainlessly:
her hands keep her busy, fluttering through each room
until all the windows are blinding.

She irons away the long afternoon,
pressing summer dresses thin as her own skin,
her face blurred by the clouds of steam.

Evening and his bedtime comes around again –
she used to kiss him, then tell him
to *Blow out the light!*

She crosses herself before falling asleep –
all night she flies for mile after starless mile
over fields of white linen.

Shifting

Once a week she feels the urge like a headache
to shift all the furniture around,
filling the house with a sound like thunder –

the red sofa lugged under the window,
the TV next to the fireplace,
the rug lengthways against the opposite wall.

It's like a Christmas cracker puzzle without a solution –
the rug this time dragged into the middle, not touching,
the TV angled towards the window,

the sofa against the wall with the radiator
that still (mental note) needs bleeding.
But there's always something that doesn't ft

something left over –
the bookcase with its shelves of green murder,
a spider plant consigned to a corner without enough light.

What doesn't change is the room, or the furniture,
only the permutations she has to work with
which may include, one of these fine days,

the TV, the bookcase, the spider plant,
the rug rolled up with its map of stains
all piled high on the badly clawed sofa,

itself shoved hard against the front door
on the other side of which a daughter,
home early from school, is pushing, pushing.

Five Easy Pieces

Of course we're on the side of the girl,
the poor, pretty, pig-ignorant and pregnant blonde
as she idles by the side of the car
waiting for Jack to pay for the gas
and get them on their way.

There she stands in her too-tight coat,
yawning and dishevelled
in the no man's land of the forecourt,
blowsy as the woman she'll become,
her back aching with eight weeks to go.

Mercifully bored, she's thinking only
that he's taking his time,
of what she might cook tonight for supper,
blind as a kitten to what's already happening to her –
which is unforgivable, and for the rest of her life.

That's where the movie always leaves her,
just before the future kicks in,
our pulses quickening as we watch him watching
as she shrinks to nothing in the truck's rear view
while the driver asks where he's from, where he's going.

The China-mender's Daughter

I want to tell her –
The people in my life are like plates,

I have to keep them happy, keep them spinning,
to ask her *Have you ever found*

the hard-fired words for pain or love
and set them ringing?

Smiling delicately, she's explaining
how he'd check for veins of damage

lifting each piece of fine-bone to the light,
how it flared, translucent,

in his fingers – a hare's ear
shot through with sun.

Muntjac

At the time it felt like a rescue –
her weight in your arms like a hero,
the lack of struggle or blood.
But now in the darkness behind your head
she is breathing quietly, and the sleep she needs
is not in your gift, no matter how gently
you take each corner like a newborn father
coming home from the ward.

Why didn't you just leave her
among the lost shoes and windshield glass,
concede, there and then, the hopelessness?
The oncoming cars dazzle and pass.
How heavy it is – this brokenness
which couldn't be helped.

To My Godmother

I thought I understood something
of the pain it caused you,
signing my name each birthday
with love
as if I could remind you
more than anything else.

I thought it was just your daughter
you missed, not seeing
that meant everything
she was missing from,
that thirty summers later
it means everything still.

Forgive me –
I did not know then
how grief works,
how it steeps the clear world
like dye from a red dress
that keeps on running.

The Edge of Something

As a child she'd lived at the edge of something –
a house backing on to open fields
rolling away under a tide of barley
towards a beech-wood where a girl could play
all summer long, out of sight and mind.

Once she'd got as far as a candle's light,
had almost reached the make-believe trees
where she'd buried her survival kit weeks before
among the roots: a penknife, half a packet
of soft digestives, the doll she'd chosen to save.

Sometimes, slipping out of bed early
while the rest of the house is curled in sleep,
she stands so still at the kitchen window
a stranger out walking in the dawning fields
might take her for a vase of wildflowers.

The Long Holidays

The day stretches ahead – nothing but
grass and sky grass and sky grass and sky grass and sky
as far as the eye can see

nothing but
sky and grass sky and grass sky and grass sky and grass

and the wind galloping hard over the fields
like a riderless horse.

As I Walked Out

Don't tell me you've never dreamed of this –
of waking in a room with a wide open window,

the air clear and ringing after night rain;
of needing no other reason than a sky

the unbelievable blue of which
sends you flitting deftly through the house

past the year-old jar of nails and flies,
the pile of dishes in the sink, and out the back door

where you're caught for an instant in the brightness
because the future's so much easier than you'd thought –

slipping your heart under the rosebush like a key,
everything you need in the canvas bag

resting lightly at your hip
and life as simple as turning left or right.

Who She Is

If you want to know who she really is
sit beside her quietly on the morning bus,

observe the way her green glass earrings
pick out the flowers in her summer dress,

then watch closely as she puts down her pen
to stare across a field of silvery brassicas.

Now imagine devouring, leaf by leaf,
each sweet and tightly folded heart.

Long Exposure

The goods have survived – the displays
of ribbons and perishables,

windows of iced patisserie,
a greengrocer's pyramid of apples.

So too, more hazily,
have those with nowhere to go –

the shoe-shine boy materialised
at the foot of his dark-suited client

or the woman sitting alone in a pavement café
with time on her hands.

Though in the light of this past
where a smile is out of the question

and the slightest gesture
makes a ghost of skin

more faithful still
is the appearance of emptiness:

a mid-morning street quiet with sun
like the moment after truth or disaster,

an absence which is really desire –
to be somewhere else

whether better or worse hardly matters
just as long as we're moving...

The Glass House

It's what you've always dreamed of:
    room after room tidal
        with light

like a mind
    that keeps on emptying itself –

by day a blue you could almost
    reach out and touch,

by night – curled soft as fruit –
    nothing between you
        and the stars.

It's where you've always lived:
    walking down the rain-glazed street
        or past the budding park –

this window which –
    like a child or bird –
        you beat your heart against:

thin and clear
    and everywhere you look.

*   *   *

What Happens While We Are Sleeping

Frost. Foxes. Owl-kills.
The wheel of stars.
Thundering lorries with somewhere
to get to by dawn.

Beads of dew forming
along the telegraph wires.
A red deer delicately eating
each closed tulip like a prayer.

Summer Storm

We wake to carpets darkened and drenched,
curtains wringing like the skirts of a heroine.

The lives we assumed would be continued
lie strewn across the garden

still shocked
by the great, blank sheets of light:

sodden tartan rugs, the scattered cushions of absent children,
bowls swimming with dashed blossom,

wine glasses filled to the brim,
a novel lying face down, swollen with rain.

I stand barefoot on the soaking grass
like the woman who walked away without a scratch.

In the sun the shirts and summer dresses hang glittering
like the clothes of the baptised.

Moonflower

Today she wakes heavy as a stone
    without knowing why

her skin chilled
    as the milk on her doorstep.

She moves through the morning's
dark circles
        like the old – slowly –
    with a sense of something forgotten.

By noon, broody for sleep, she succumbs
    climbing back into bed
sheets wide as a field.

The pollen freckling her arms
    the grass-seed threading the hem
of her nightdress

      are easily missed.
She sinks deep without dreaming

(only last night
a moth mistook her throat
for a flower)

Hide Nor Hair

By lunchtime the fields and private woods should be echoing,
the doors of barns and outbuildings dragged open,
their rusted machinery exposed to the sun.
By dusk it should be serious as the river.

It takes until nightfall to become a dream –
the creak of dark stairs, the back door sticking
for the last time, that ring of mushrooms on the green
blooming in the moonlight like a soul.

Harvest

For once when you ask
I follow without question,

brushing past the sour nettles
that choke the gap in the hawthorn hedge

to stand at the edge of this moment
you have led us to:

full and clear
it rises like music over the wheat.

Far off a back-yard dog
starts barking at the stars

and is answered in kind –
We are this far apart but not alone.

Across the bone dry fields
a farmhouse window is shining like home

as a light will always shine
when seen from a great enough distance.

Garbo Among Us

She could be this woman you hold a glass door
open for, not because she's beautiful but old;

or perhaps you brushed shoulders with her fur
as you hurried along the crowded winter street;

or that pale-faced girl you stopped to ask for directions,
didn't she speak as if her words were a commandment

to leave this world entirely –
carry on to the end, then keep on walking?

Wherever you go it may be that you're touched
without knowing it, strangely and lightly

as a flurry of snow in the night
touches the stone kings and rough sleepers.

The Promise of Snow

Why risk setting out at this late hour,
leaving the glow of the city behind,

the good roads dwindling to little more than a track
on its tortuous climb through the mountains?

Why heed that old tug of the blood,
the skin's first inkling as the mercury dips

that tonight the white horse is flying,
covering the ground between here and the past

if it weren't on the off-chance
that you were already braving the dark

to meet me again at that gap in the sky
where we stood, open-mouthed, to catch the first wafers?

Things Left Out All Night

acquire a gravitas –

the spade presiding over rows of lettuces
grown solemn as a cross

the white sheet worn thin by dreams
still glimmering with stars...

as if something had come to pass –

a trowel, half-sunk in earth,
patient as rust

the wheelbarrow stood in long grass
absolved by rain.

*   *   *

Homing

You could hold it in your hand –
this all encompassing desire
housed in a few ounces of feather and bone,

the distance between release –
nights of mountainous cold and hunger –
and a known darkness

where something close to love might stand
shaking the pan of grain
and calling softly.

Short-hold

This is the gap before territory,
    before the first fight, the first sex.

The black cat knows it, twitching his tail
    on the wrong lawn.

This is the time when our luck might stray –
    the syllable *flit* swoops through the trees,

leaves behind reminder
    after red reminder.

Even this lamplight's provisional,
    tomorrow may shine from a different window;

our lives are still fragile
    wrapped in old headlines and stars.

How empty the white bookshelves are,
    how easily tipped...

weightless the walls of clocks, pictures, mirrors...
    I stand at the open door, calling...

Meanwhile you've lit the difficult boiler.
    All night its steady breathing fills the kitchen

like the sleep of a new-born
    we haven't yet named.

Wayfarer

People always think they belong somewhere,
some patch of earth claims them more than any other,
but his feet have always told him otherwise,
settling for a few days here or there by chance –
a kind word at the right moment,
a dry barn with no lock on the door,
a farmer with a blind eye.

But for weeks now he's been showing up
every day to tend this garden –
weeding, dead-heading, mowing the grass –
small tasks that somehow
keep coming around.
A neighbour's lent a caravan and a yard,
someone else donates a telly

and suddenly he's been here long enough
to see the runner's scarlet flowers
turn into beans, to eat them,
steaming, from a bowl with butter.
Part of the furniture! they pull his leg
pouring him another glass of red
that tastes of the ground it came from.

It still feels strange for him to say goodnight,
and walk back up the lane
to where?
'Home' is the wrong word
but what else to call it –
this blue glow from his window
spilling out across the open fields?

Still Life with Purple Sage

Where is the woman
whose kitchen this is,

whose hands arranged these spoons
with their worn silver edges?

I want to tell her how patiently
her life is waiting,

the bread knife catching the light
like a meaning,

the thin-stemmed glass
full of the breath it was blown with.

The window's wide open –
perhaps she's in the garden

bruising a leaf of purple sage
between her fingers

wondering what to cook tonight
or if she'll stay?

At the Falls Café

Think of me as the waitress
serving drinks at the Falls Café,
who carries chinking tumblers of iced water
on a tilting silver tray above her head
as she threads the crowds of tourists,

always watching over that solitary guest
who lets the skin grow on his coffee,
whose fingers shred white serviettes,
or circle the edge of his bitter cup,
whose gaze is lost in the rainbows and mist.

Think of my touch
as the hand laid softly on your shoulder
that returns you, blinking, back to earth:
to the unbroken rolls on your table,
this red I invite you now to taste.

After Life

As far back as great, great, great
    names and faces
        are scoured away

like plates scraped clean
    of painted flowers
        by daughters wanting more.

What remains
    after voice and gesture are lost,
        is less love

than force of habit:
    the angle of a peeler's
        thinning blade,

the battered wisdom of the pan
    you boil the morning milk in,
        its patina of burnt lace.

If only I could learn to be
    this fit for purpose:
        the passed-down smoothness

of handled ash, a dailyness
    like prayer or bread
        and the mouth's need of them.

Spare Room in Summer

A private arrangement
between these white walls
and the sun slanting in like a thought:

So this is what the world looks like
when I am not here:

The light hasn't caught me yet,
is too absorbed

persuading each simple object
of its existence:

the slipware bowl, its creaminess,
the rosewood, its glow.

A door handle gleams
like the foot of an icon
rubbed into brightness.

It's like being a child again,
the fever gone
but kept home from school one more day,

the coolness of my mother's other life
as she airs each room of our dreams.

Detail

It may be that somewhere else
more important things are at stake:
    angels and infantas,
    robes and raiment,
    a haloed revelation
    with uplifted hands,
that the truth's already blazing away,
a woman's life is being changed for good.

I'd rather put my faith
in a light like this:
    the chastening glaze
    of a china cup
    set against a pewter dish
    the colour of an overcast sky;
its delicate and sobering touch
as if remembering the face of a loved one
who ate at this table daily.

This Morning

I watched the sun moving round the kitchen,
an early spring sun that strengthened and weakened,
coming and going like an old mind.

I watched like one bedridden for a long time
on their first journey back into the world
who finds it enough to be going on with:

the way the sunlight brought each possession in turn
to its attention and made of it a small still life:

the iron frying pan gleaming on its hook like an ancient find,
the powdery green cheek of a bruised clementine.

Though more beautiful still was how the light moved on,
letting go each chair and coffee cup without regret

the way my grandmother, in her final year, received me:
neither surprised by my presence, nor distressed by my leaving,
content, though, while I was there.

Last Summer

I want to come back as sunlight
to steal over everything I own

with the warmth of skin
that isn't there.

I want to concentrate:
to fill each room for an hour

as if the house were a kind of clock
without hands or a face.

I want to shine with a disinterest
approaching love

on the life laid aside
so hastily this morning:

the flowered dress discarded
as too last-summer

this book I've been reading
to get me to sleep.

Woman in Blue Reading a Letter

It could be love that's brought you here –

to stand at this window
with your unlined face
tilting a future towards the light

that's clear as white spirit.
Outside time is sliding by
like ice on the river,

but this stillness is a ring
you might keep forever
in a silk-lined box,

the air redolent of beeswax,
life humming faintly in the rooms beyond
like a rumour of summer.

You may never be happier
dressed in your scrap of cloudless sky
holding the words

you've been sent from somewhere else.

*

If I could I'd step into
    this dimension of light,

become the woman who stands alone at its centre
    casting no shadow,

whose unreadable face
    is so absorbed in the world of her letter

she doesn't notice how close
    this moment is to heaven:

a tender geometry
    of walls and air

where her body is held forever,
    clothed in the blue of hyacinth and distance,

where even the spaces between things
    are part of the meaning.

*

You've lived so long inside this room
it's become your world –

the lustre of discarded pearls,
the softer sheen of satin and skin

more real to you now than food or debts,
the boatman's distant cries on the river.

No wonder you hesitate
before lifting the tip of your brush

for the very last time.
It will feel like stepping out of a dream –

the light streaming untroubled
from its invisible source,

and the woman you wrapped in lapis
lost in her thoughts,

the love unfolding without you.

Guest Room

Whatever you thought you wanted here –
clean sheets, nail scissors, book –

has slipped your mind completely
like the name of a cousin at a wedding

three times removed.
The trick is not trying to remember,

to hover in the doorway at a loss,
a visitor among the things of the world.

There will be no words
for what comes back to you then –

call it a kind of stillness, rarely entered,
which might be its own reward

like the scent in a drawer of folded scarves,
or a bed not slept in since winter.

Morandi: Still Lives

In the same year the tide of war turns
    a porcelain bowl nestles, lip to foot,
        against the milky glaze of a favourite bottle;
the balance of power tips
    depending on whether the rusted enamel pitcher
        is painted facing left or right.
Sometime in the early sixties
    a candlestick takes a vow of silence.

Always the eye and the hand remain constant
    inside this small room with its shelves of bric-à-brac
    and one source of light;
a white vase with its cargo of roses
    still carries on voyaging
        towards the edge of the known world.

The Dew Artist

Perhaps it's enough that someone thought of it:
of rising in the gap between night workers coming home

and the first dawn commuters,
to stand barefoot on a canvas of grass

brushing the knap patiently forwards and back
like a finger marking the softness of baize or suede

before shouldering the broom through the tall city streets
past the boy bleary-eyed behind all-night glass,

the nurse finishing her shift in intensive care
as the moon fades.

Perhaps it makes no difference
if the pattern burns into mist

long before the woman out walking her dog
within the roar of the bypass

has had time to glimpse the impossible:
perfect circles arrived at

through a concurrence of water and light
glittering the earth's surface like a dream,

if we believe they've been prepared –
those small green spaces

where we gather in our lunch hours on warm days
to sit and eat

or, loosening our ties, lie back with eyes closed
on the common or garden.

The Messengers

Babies are, so too the newly dead,
sometimes also the drivers of tinted cars.
Others we know by name, though more often than not

the future's an officer removing his hat
as we answer the door.

What they deliver in words and flesh
is irreversible –

a woman pegging out bed linen
hears the phone ring and goes inside,
not knowing that, by the time she returns,

the weather will have broken,
the sheets left flapping on the line for days.

Awkward, casual, oblivious,
appearing out of the blue
or leaving a note wedged in the crack of a table,

they give us our lives,
the ones we know at the end of them
by how they've been mended.

This is true even of the man dressed in white
who faces the woman with gauze at her throat.

In a moment he'll give her the news,
he will send her out changed and astonished
into the radiant world.

Mrs Meakin Opens Her Window to the Larks

It takes her back to a morning years before,
shaking out the dust from an upstairs window
after hours of indoor toiling –

the same sense of leaning into a blue
which seemed, like the spiralling arias,
to carry on forever

and her own wide-armed gesture like a farewell
as if, on the spur of that moment,
she'd let herself go.

Early One Morning

(for Douglas's Grandmother)

As he spoke you rose up
in your light cotton dress,

came walking towards us
out of a valley of brood mares and fevers,

carrying your case
with its one change of clothes,

the price of a week's lodgings
tucked in your purse

and beyond that a future
you'd never have dreamed:

its hills still misty
at this hour of the day

and somewhere, two wars
and four daughters away,

here I am listening
as you turn into song.

To Manor Farm Only

Halfway between two sleepy villages
a fingerpost points across a meadow

empty of the cattle that lowed for a week
until they forgot grass.

Now their milky faces loom dreamily
through the bars of their hay racks.

Frost in the hollows,
the path curving down towards a small river

where, hidden from view among willows,
there must be a footbridge just wide enough

and after that, another mile or two perhaps
through fields flooding blue at this hour,

the stars moving in their slow herds
as you leave the last gate open.

Verses

*And there followed him a certain
young man, having a linen cloth cast
about his naked body; and the young
men laid hold on him:
   And he left the linen cloth, and
fled from them naked.*

ST MARK'S GOSPEL, CH. 14, V. 51-52

Who are you, young man
without a name
whose tender curiosity leads you,
pale and shivering, every spring
to the edge of passion?

No one knows, not even the writer
who couldn't quite bring himself to edit you out
though you play no further part in the story,
your life before and after
blank as the sheet you leave behind.

And yet a ditch of cow parsley,
a patch of moonlight or bed linen
glimmering on a washing line
and here you are again, haring off
across the garden, naked and older.

*

My grandmother once told me how,
in a more innocent time,
the farmer would drive up to the hill top field
and shine his headlamps full
into the ripening wheat

until, through the warm summer night,
the courting couples began to appear,
rising up hand in hand
and walking towards the brightness shyly
as if out of a parable or dream.

The Gardener

This time of year again –
doing the work we must bend to or kneel,

like the man rising at evening
from the furrows he's been digging all day,

his hands muddy with planting,
patting the earth tenderly into place

around each nameless seed.
Along the lane, the rain-washed body

of a hare, blackthorn flowering overnight.
Time to be turning in he thinks

as he gazes at a sowing of early stars
with eyes just the colour you remember.

Ridgeway

You are given this day – the road curving
empty and white in the sun, the sky a larkspur blue.

For the next few hours
the world will be utterly free from meaning,

a stone you kick for a mile
along a track that's hard, but isn't like bone.

No one will ask you to heal them or show them the way.
No one will bring you their dead.

It doesn't matter if what you are walking towards
is heavy as bread – each day broken

in your own two hands
as the earth is broken spring after spring –

only that you are walking
through the fields of young wheat,

your spirit as light
as the eggshell you spot in the grass,

or the wind singing
over Blowing-Stone Hill.

*   *   *

Risen

Like the woman who wakes at dawn
to find herself three fields from home
my body is given to me like a flower –

the kind that stars the hedgerow every spring,
the kind I used to pick as a child
without thinking.

Perhaps if I keep very still and empty
I too will grow into stem, leaf, corona,
become the common wayside name for love.

The thought opens up in this early morning light
with such a wild sweetness
it could fill the whole house for a day.

NOTES

Among Women (10) and **Blessed Art Thou** (16): These titles come from the story of the Annunciation as told in St Luke's Gospel, Ch. 1, v. 28: 'And the angel came in unto her, and said, Hail, thou that art highly favoured, the Lord is with thee: blessed art thou among women.'

Enola Gay (19): This Boeing B-29 Superfortress bomber became the first aircraft to drop an atomic bomb as a weapon of war when, on 6 August 1945, it targeted the city of Hiroshima, Japan. The plane was named after Enola Gay Tibbets, mother of Paul Tibbets, the mission's pilot.

Five Easy Pieces (21): A film directed by Bob Rafelson in 1970 and starring Jack Nicholson as a dropout from upper-class America.

Woman in Blue Reading a Letter (49): The title of a famous painting by the Dutch master, Johannes Vermeer (1632-75).

Morandi: Still Lives (52): Giorgio Morandi (1890-1964) was an Italian artist who specialised in still lives. Known as 'il monaco', the monk, due to his reclusive lifestyle, he famously limited his choice of still life objects to the unremarkable bottles, boxes, jars, jugs and vases that were commonly found in his everyday domestic environment.

Mrs Meakin Opens Her Window to the Larks (55): The title of a painting by Mary Newcomb (1922-2008) who spent much of her artistic life in Suffolk.

Early One Morning (56): The title of a well-known English folk tune dating back to the 18th century.